U.S. HISTORY IN REVIEW

THE PANAMA CANAL

Emmett Martin

Enslow PUBLISHING

Please visit our website, www.enslow.com. For a free color catalog of all our high-quality books, call toll free 1-800-398-2504 or fax 1-877-980-4454.

Portions of this work were originally authored by Marie Roesser and published as *The Panama Canal*. All new material this edition authored by Emmett Martin.

Cataloging-in-Publication Data
Names: Martin, Emmett.
Title: The Panama Canal / Emmett Martin.
Description: Buffalo, NY : Enslow Publishing, 2027. | Series: U.S. History in review | Includes glossary.
Identifiers: ISBN 9781978547131 (pbk.) | ISBN 9781978547148 (library bound) | ISBN 9781978547155 (ebook)
Subjects: LCSH: Panama Canal (Panama)–History–Juvenile literature. | Canals–Panama–Juvenile literature. | Panama Canal (Panama)–Juvenile literature. | Panama Canal (Panama)–Design and construction–Juvenile literature.
Classification: LCC TC745.M327 2027 | DDC 972.875–dc23

Published in 2027 by
Enslow Publishing
2544 Clinton Street
Buffalo, NY 14224

Designer: Leslie Taylor
Interior layout: Tanya Dellaccio Keeney
Editor: Therese Shea

Photo credits: Series art (grunge flag) Andrey Kuzmin/Shutterstock.com; series art (stamp icon) Stocker_team/Shutterstock.com; series art (font) santstock/Shutterstock.com; series art (swash) BUTENKOV ALEKSEI/Shutterstock.com; cover Courtesy of the Library of Congress; p. 5 Jose Mario Espinoza/Shutterstock.com; p. 7 Monika Hunackova/Shutterstock.com; p. 9 https://upload.wikimedia.org/wikipedia/commons/2/2f/The_Panama_Canal_-_The_Great_Culebra_Cut.jpg; p. 11 (top) https://upload.wikimedia.org/wikipedia/commons/3/33/AGHRC_(1890)_-_Carta_XIII_-_División_política_de_Colombia,_1886.jpg; p. 11 (bottom) https://upload.wikimedia.org/wikipedia/commons/8/82/1870_Nicaragua_Canal_Map_Restoration.png; p. 13 (top) https://upload.wikimedia.org/wikipedia/commons/5/5b/Theodore_Roosevelt_by_the_Pach_Bros.jpg; p. 13 (bottom) https://upload.wikimedia.org/wikipedia/commons/4/4e/MarioModel90_1908.jpg; p. 15 https://upload.wikimedia.org/wikipedia/commons/4/49/Panama_Canal_under_construction%2C_1907.jpg; p. 17 https://upload.wikimedia.org/wikipedia/commons/a/a8/William_Crawford_Gorgas_Scientific_Monthly.jpg; p. 19 https://upload.wikimedia.org/wikipedia/commons/0/0f/Roosevelt_and_the_Canal.JPG; p. 21 Glasshouse Images/Alamy Images; p. 23 (top) KGPA Ltd/Alamy Images; p. 23 (bottom) https://upload.wikimedia.org/wikipedia/commons/5/5a/SS_Ancon_entering_west_chamber_cph.3b17471u.jpg; p. 25 Peter Hermes Furian/Shutterstock.com; p. 27 https://upload.wikimedia.org/wikipedia/commons/d/d1/Agua_Clara_Locks_09_2019_0822.jpg; p. 29 Jose Mario Espinoza/Shutterstock.com.

Printed in the United States of America

CPSIA compliance information: Batch #CSENS27: For further information, contact Enslow Publishing, New York, New York, at 1-800-398-2504.

Contents

Words in the glossary appear in ***bold*** *the first time they are used in the text.*

A World Wonder

The Panama Canal is one of the Seven Wonders of the Modern World. This waterway in Central America was created in the early 1900s. It's about 40 miles (64 km) long and connects the Atlantic and Pacific Oceans. It changed the world.

Learn More

A canal is a long narrow waterway made by people. Canals are created for boat travel. They also bring water to or from a place.

A Long Journey

Before the Panama Canal, boats traveling from the East Coast of the United States to the West Coast had to go all the way around South America. From New York City to San Francisco, California, that's about 13,000 miles (20,920 km). Using the canal cut that trip to about 5,000 miles (8,047 km).

Learn More

Ships carrying goods from Europe to the west coast of the Americas or East Asia also had to go around South America. This trip was both long and dangerous.

First Thoughts

In the 1500s, Spanish explorers thought about building a canal to connect the Atlantic and Pacific Oceans. They thought the **Isthmus** of Panama would be an ideal place to do it. However, digging through mountains and forests proved to be a hard job. The French were the first to try but failed.

Learn More

A French company tried to build a canal across Panama in the late 1800s. They gave up by 1889 because of diseases, or illnesses, and other problems. About 22,000 workers died.

French construction, 1885

An American Effort

In 1902, the United States offered to take over the building of the canal from the French company. However, the land where the canal was being built belonged to Colombia at that time. The Colombian government wouldn't agree to sell the land to the United States.

Colombia, 1890

Learn More

Before 1902, the United States had been planning a canal through the wider country of Nicaragua, which is north of Panama.

plan for a Nicaragua canal

A Nation Forms

In 1903, some Panamanians decided to declare Panama a free country, independent of Colombia. U.S. president Theodore Roosevelt sent armed forces to help their **revolution**. The new government of Panama let the United States buy the land for the canal.

Theodore Roosevelt

Learn More

The United States agreed to pay Panama $10 million for the canal land. (This is like paying $36 billion today.) The United States also agreed to pay $250,000 for the use of the canal every year after.

A Difficult Start

Canal construction didn't go well at first. The tools the United States had bought from France worked poorly. Many workers became sick with the diseases called **yellow fever** and **malaria**. The chief **engineer** quit after a year.

Learn More

Around 1900, scientists discovered malaria and yellow fever spread through **mosquito** bites.

canal construction, 1907

Deadly Diseases

U.S. army doctor William Gorgas became a leader in the fight against disease at the construction site. Gorgas had the water taken out of nearby ponds and lakes because mosquitoes lay eggs in still bodies of water. He made sure houses and buildings had screens. New hospitals were built as well.

Dr. William Gorgas

Learn More

Dr. Gorgas's plans dropped the number of cases of yellow fever and malaria.

Back to Work

Construction began under the United States in 1904. Some worked with shovels. Others used cranes, drills, and **dynamite**. Huge machines dug into the earth and lifted dirt into railroad cars, which took the dirt away. **Concrete** was poured within the canal's locks.

President Roosevelt in a steam shovel, 1907

Learn More

Natural events, including floods and an **earthquake**, made building the Panama Canal even harder.

Canal Locks

Locks needed to be built in the canal so boats wouldn't get stuck. Locks work a bit like steps. When a boat moves into a lock, gates close. Water comes in or out to raise or lower the boat. Then, the boat moves to the next lock.

Learn More

Around the middle of the canal locks is Gatún Lake, a human-made body of water. It's more than 80 feet (24 m) above sea level.

A Dynamite Finish

President Woodrow Wilson finished the canal—from Washington, DC! On October 10, 1913, Wilson pressed a **telegraph** button in the White House. The signal set off dynamite at the canal site, about 4,000 miles (6,437 km) away. Water rushed into the canal. The canal opened for boats August 15, 1914.

Learn More

The canal was the costliest construction project in U.S. history up to that point, about $380 million.

dynamite at canal site, 1913

the first ship to enter the Panama Canal, the SS *Ancon*

Wanted: Water

The Panama Canal needs a large amount of water to operate its locks. Each vessel requires around 48 million gallons (182 million l) of water to travel the entire path. Most of this water comes from Gatún Lake. A dam at one end of the Chagres River created this lake.

Learn More

Gatún Lake is also a source of drinking water for Panama City and Colón, Panama.

Taking Turns

Between 13,000 and 14,000 ships use the canal each year, or about 44 vessels a day. The trip takes between 8 and 10 hours. Big ships pay between tens of thousands of dollars to hundreds of thousands of dollars. Sometimes they wait days for a turn through the canal.

Learn More

In 1999, the United States gave control of the canal to Panama.

Still a Wonder

As shipping vessels have changed over the years, the Panama Canal has had to make changes too. Channels have been widened and deepened to allow larger ships to pass through. In 2016, Panama created new locks for the largest ships. The canal continues to be one of the world's most important waterways.

Learn More

In 2023, a **drought** caused ships to get stuck in the canal. Some waited weeks to pass through.

A Timeline of the Panama Canal

1882
A French company begins building a canal across today's Panama.

1889
The French stop digging the canal due to the cost and lives lost.

1903
Panama declares independence from Columbia.

1904
The United States buys control of the canal land from Panama and begins work.

1905
Dr. William Gorgas leads the effort to fight malaria and yellow fever near the canal site.

1914
The canal opens for ships.

1999
Panama takes control of the canal from the United States.

2016
A third set of locks is completed in the Panama Canal for larger ships.

Glossary

concrete: A hard, strong matter used for building and made by mixing cement, sand, and broken rocks with water.

drought: A long period of very dry weather.

dynamite: A powerful explosive, which is matter that causes a great blast.

earthquake: A shaking of the ground caused by the movement of Earth's crust.

engineer: One who plans and builds machines.

isthmus: A narrow piece of land that connects two larger pieces of land.

malaria: An illness that causes chills and fever and is passed through mosquito bites.

mosquito: A small fly that feeds on blood and can spread illness.

revolution: A movement to overthrow a government.

telegraph: A method of communicating using electric signals sent through wires.

yellow fever: An illness that causes fever and yellowish skin that can be passed through mosquito bites.

For More Information

Books

Rossiter, Brienna. *Panama Canal*. Mendota Heights, MN: Apex Editions, 2024.

Silva, Sadie. *Panama*. New York, NY: Cavendish Square Publishing, 2022.

Website

U.S. History: Panama Canal
www.ducksters.com/history/us_1900s/panama_canal.php
Read more interesting facts about this marvel in engineering.

Publisher's note to educators and parents: *Our editors have carefully reviewed these websites to ensure that they are suitable for students. Many websites change frequently, however, and we cannot guarantee that a site's future contents will continue to meet our high standards of quality and educational value. Be advised that students should be closely supervised whenever they access the internet.*

Index